# NEW BOOKS FOR NEW READERS

## Judy Cheatham
*General Editor*

D0830465

Algonquin Area Public Library
2600 Harnish Dr.
Algonquin, IL 60102
www.aapld.org

# History Mysteries

The Cases of James Harrod, Tecumseh,
"Honest Dick" Tate, and William Goebel

*James C. Klotter*

THE UNIVERSITY PRESS OF KENTUCKY

The New Books for New Readers project was made possible through funding from the National Endowment for the Humanities, the Kentucky Humanities Council, and *The Kentucky Post.* The opinions expressed in this book are not necessarily those of the Kentucky Humanities Council.

Scholarly publisher for the Commonwealth,
serving Bellarmine University, Berea College, Centre College of Kentucky, Eastern Kentucky University, The Filson Historical Society, Georgetown College, Kentucky Historical Society, Kentucky State University, Morehead State University, Murray State University, Northern Kentucky University, Transylvania University, University of Kentucky, University of Louisville, and Western Kentucky University.
All rights reserved.

*Editorial and Sales Offices:* The University Press of Kentucky
663 South Limestone Street, Lexington, Kentucky 40508-4008
www.kentuckypress.com

15 14 13 12 11    10 9 8 7 6

Library of Congress Cataloging-in-Publication Data

Klotter, James C.
    History mysteries: the cases of James Harrod, Tecumseh, "Honest Dick" Tate, and William Goebel / James C. Klotter
        p. cm.—(New books for new readers)
    ISBN-10: 0-8131-0903-5
    1. Kentucky—History—Miscellanea. 2. Curiosities and wonders—Kentucky—History. 3. Readers for new literates.
I. Title. II. Series.
F451.5.K58  1989
976.9—dc20
ISBN-13: 978-0-8131-0903-9

This book is printed on acid-free paper meeting the requirements of the American National Standard for Permanence in Paper for Printed Library Materials.

Manufactured in the United States of America.

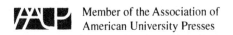

Member of the Association of
American University Presses

# Acknowledgments

To learn about a subject, an author reads those books already written about that subject. In my case, I owe a great debt to the authors listed in the "Other Readings" section of the bibliography. Their work made my task much easier. An author also produces a better book if it is read carefully by good editors. This work has benefited from readings by Judy Cheatham and my wife, Freda Campbell Klotter. Cheryl Conover, James Russell Harris, Mary Lou Madigan, Mary Winter, and others at the Kentucky Historical Society aided in various ways as well. Ramona Lumpkin and the Kentucky Humanities Council, the Scripps-Howard Foundation, the National Endowment for the Humanities, the Kentucky Department for Libraries and Archives, the Kentucky Literacy Commission, and the University Press of Kentucky—all deserve much praise for their support of the overall project. Finally, I wish to thank Sandra Schneider of the Shelby County Public Library and the real advisors on this book—the new readers of the Shelby County and Henry County literacy programs: Mary Frances Beach, Jo Brewer, Jenny Cole, Susan Crouch, Frances Dennie, Irene Duvall, Sue Flowers, Mary Frazier, Ron Horseman, Della Howard, Elaine Johnson, Gloria Jean Jones, Alma Lacefield, Jerry Mahan, Kouen Moeur, Thalmen Moeur, Carol Montgomery, Wakely Purple, Sandra Redmon, James Stone, and Terry Watson. They taught this Ph.D. a lot.

# The Historian as Detective

History is a record of what has taken place in the past. Studying that history can be a great deal of fun, for the action is all real. No one is making up the story. The people *did* live and the events *did* happen. We can learn so much from these people of the past—from their mistakes, from their successes.

A person who writes that history is called a historian. One author has said that a historian is really a kind of detective. That part of history is what this book is all about.

In a mystery book or movie, the detective is looking for clues to solve a crime. Historians use clues, too. Historians are seeking to find out all they can about something that happened earlier. Just like detectives, these historians have to decide which clues are good ones and which ones are not. Then historians have to put all their clues together and write about the people and events of the past.

This book presents four real mysteries. You, the reader, will be given clues so you can be a historian—and detective—too. Perhaps you can decide what happened in each case. Or perhaps these mysteries will remain unsolved. That is the fun of history.

Let's go back into Kentucky's past and explore its many mysteries.

# The Disappearance of James Harrod

In the year 1792, Kentucky became a state. Its
frontier days were over. That same year a tall, rough,
good-looking man with black hair and fierce dark eyes
got ready to go on a hunting trip. His name was James
Harrod. Harrod had led the first settlers into Kentucky,
even before Daniel Boone. The town of Harrodsburg
had been named for him. Harrod had fought the
Indians. He had also helped make Kentucky a state.

But now Harrod lived at peace and loved to relax and
hunt in far-off woods. Often he would be gone for
months at a time. For this hunt, he put on a linen shirt
with silver buttons. He placed his hat, made of beaver
fur, on his head, and picked up his old rifle. Harrod
said good-bye to his wife, Ann, and their seven-year-old
daughter. Then he left. Ann and the little girl would
not see him again.

Harrod and two other men went up the Kentucky
River into the eastern part of the state. They said they
were hunting for beaver. But some other people thought
they were looking for a secret silver mine. Years before,
a man named Swift had told of finding such a place.
But he had gone to England and was put in jail there.
By the time Swift came back to Kentucky he was blind
and could not find the mine again. Or so his story
went. Many people had looked for the mine since
then. But no one ever found it.

9

Perhaps Harrod was only hunting. Or maybe he was searching for lost silver. Whatever he was doing, problems arose.

James Harrod was never heard from again.

An early writer said, "Nothing is known as to the manner of his death." But is that true? Who was this man, James Harrod? What was his life like? What *is* known about his disappearance? Can the mystery be solved now, after all these years?

Just what happened to James Harrod?

Like most mysteries, the clues go back many years. Even James Harrod's own life is a mystery. We do not know when he was born. Some say about 1746. Others give other dates. No written record gives his date of birth.

We do not even know if Harrod could read or write. Some people said he could not. Since that time, however, letters of his have been found. They show that Harrod could write. He also kept good records of his army service. His house had seven "old books" in it at one time. So Harrod may not have been able to read or write very well. But he could do both.

Many of the details of Harrod's early life are almost unknown, too. His father died before James was ten years old. The widow raised a dozen children near the border of Maryland and Pennsylvania. But one day his mother quickly placed some of her family on a horse.

The rest walked. They left their home because they feared an Indian attack. From a hill, they saw the attack. Their home was burned. James heard the cries of dying friends. This was not Harrod's last brush with Indians.

All this took place before the Revolutionary War. America was still part of England. When England fought the French and Indians in a war, the Americans joined in. James Harrod served as one of those fighters. He was only about 14 years old but he fought in several battles before the war ended 3 years later.

It was now peaceful for a time. People like Harrod grew restless. They wanted to know about the land to the west. What lay across the hills and down the Ohio River? What was this empty, rich land like? What was this place called Kentucky?

At first, Harrod went into what is now the state of Illinois. He lived with French traders and learned their language. Harrod then stayed for a time with the Indians of that area. He could also speak with them before he left. And he brought back many furs for sale. It had been a good trip.

Some time later, Harrod made another visit out west. On this trip he met an old friend, Daniel Boone. The two talked, then went their own ways. Harrod hunted and then went home by boat on the Ohio River. He had seen Kentucky, but he could not forget it.

Over the next years, Harrod made many more trips to Kentucky. Sometimes he hunted. Other times he looked for good land to live on later. Settlers would arrive in only a matter of time.

By 1774, America and England were near war. Two years later the Declaration of Independence would be written. But the western part of America seemed more interested in this new land—Kentucky.

For people who were poor and had little land, Kentucky gave hope. Stories about the place made it sound like heaven. Great buffalo herds roamed the land. Elk, deer, turkeys, and all kinds of other animals lived there and could be hunted for food. Large trees covered the earth. Huge beech and oak and others could be used for building homes. Clear streams and many rivers meant water would not be a problem.

The soil itself was so rich that the early settlers were amazed. Giant cane, all kinds of grasses, and later big corn crops made Kentucky seem like a Garden of Eden. It was heaven on Earth.

But that heaven had another side. One Indian name for Kentucky meant "dark and bloody ground." The area might be a rich land, but it was also a dangerous land. No Indian tribe lived there. But many hunted that land. The Indians would not give up their hunting grounds.

James Harrod knew a lot about Kentucky in 1774.

He knew of its rich soil. He knew of its dangers as well. But he made up his mind to settle this land. That year he and some 50 men left for Kentucky. The men voted Harrod as their leader. These men came down the Ohio River, then went upstream on the Kentucky River. They stopped and left their boats. They walked on an old buffalo road for a few miles and made camp near a spring.

There they made the first permanent settlement in Kentucky. Harrod and his men built cabins. They planted crops. Each man got part of the land as his own. This place had several names but it grew to be called Harrodsburg. The men had liked their leader. They honored him by naming the town after him.

Harrod picked some rich land about six miles away for his land claim. He named the area Boiling Springs. He cut the brush there. Then he marked the place so people would know it was his. He began building a cabin. Most of these homes had a fireplace but no windows. They had one room and a heavy door. At night a big crossbar would be placed over that door to lock it.

The settlers needed such strong cabins because of the danger of Indian attacks. They always had to be careful. Back in the East, red men and white were fighting. Daniel Boone and another man were sent to warn Harrod. Boone warned him, then built a cabin and claimed some land. The men at Harrodsburg watched for Indians, but none came. Then one day some hunters were cooking their breakfast. Indians surprised them and killed one man. The rest of the hunters fled.

Harrod and his men went into their cabins for safety. They waited for an attack. But the Indians left. Harrod, now called "Captain Jim," led some men out to bury the dead man. Harrod decided that he did not have enough people with him to protect the area. He and his men left their cabins and all went back to the East. They would have to try again.

The next year Harrod and his men got ready to return to Kentucky. They built boats and put supplies in them. The men had guns, powder, bullets, and axes. They loaded food, salt, pots, and pans. Everything had to be taken with them, for there were no stores in Kentucky.

They went down the Ohio River again and made their way back to the cabins they had left the year before. A short time later Daniel Boone led a group of men through the Wilderness Road and set up his fort. It was called Boonesborough. A third group of people started building homes at Logan's Fort, near what is today Stanford. The settlement of Kentucky had started. In only 17 years it would become a state.

But before statehood could happen, much blood would be shed. Many hard days lay ahead. To protect themselves, the men built a fort. Few lived there except when an attack seemed near. Life in the fort was crowded and dusty. The water supply was dirty, since dead animals and filth from the fort washed into it. But the people needed safety.

Women and children joined the men that fall. The fort was made stronger over the months. A schoolhouse was built inside. For a time the area was quiet. Then, in 1777, Indians killed a man and took his scalp. They killed the cows and other livestock. People went into the fort for safety. Harrod and other men would slip out at night to hunt for food.

On one of those hunting trips Harrod heard a rifle ball go near the black hair that fell to his shoulders. He hid and put his hat on the end of his rifle. He lifted up the hat. The Indians fired. Harrod saw one Indian and shot him. Then he shot a second. Harrod got away and rode back to the fort. In fact, James Harrod would never be hurt in a fight with Indians.

In those times of danger the people looked to Harrod, for he was a natural leader. Over six feet tall— very tall for that time—he was strong and brave. Harrod could shoot very well. But most people liked him because he helped others. If people needed food, he would bring them a deer. He did not brag about his actions. Harrod could be gentle, quiet, and almost shy—except when people needed a leader. Then he might show a strong temper. Harrod was probably happiest when he was in the woods alone. He had simple needs and liked the open air and freedom best of all.

But James Harrod could not hunt in the woods as much as he liked, for he had other duties. He was a colonel in the local armed forces. And by 1778, he was married. Ann Coburn had married a man named McDonald and had moved to Kentucky with him. Soon after, McDonald was killed by Indians. Ann's father was also killed and scalped. The widow and her one-year-old son stayed on in Kentucky and lived at Logan's Fort.

With so few women around, the pretty, well-dressed widow began to have many callers. She was only 22 years old. James Harrod met her, courted her, and soon married her. He was 34, handsome, and wealthy. At their wedding, the two probably had a dinner of buffalo, bear, or deer meat, then a big party. Weddings gave people some fun in their drab days. A lot of drinking would take place, and men and women would dance into the night. Then they would go home and try to build their own lives in this wilderness.

Harrod and his wife seemed very happy. They moved from his farm to Harrodsburg for her safety. But they still took chances. One time they and 24 other people left to go to Louisville, where George Rogers Clark was giving a dance. But they saw Indians, so the Harrods and the rest went back to the fort. The next day a smaller group started again and made it. James and Ann Harrod danced the first jig and had a good time before they returned.

Such good times were rare. Even the weather seemed to be trying to drive people from Kentucky. The winter of 1779-1780 was so bad that people always called it the "Hard Winter." Snow stood on the ground for months. The cold was the worst anyone could recall. The Ohio River froze over. The Kentucky River had ice two feet thick on it. A man at that time wrote, "The hogs were frozen to death, the deer, not able to get water or food, were found dead in great numbers." Many animals died, and their cries filled the night. Maple trees cracked as their sap froze until they burst open. People had frostbite. Some died from the cold and from lack of food. Yet the people stayed. They had fought too hard to give up now.

As each year passed after that winter, things got better for the people of Kentucky. Crops grew well. More men and women came to the area, and there was safety in numbers. Stores opened. There were fewer Indian fights—except for one sad year. In 1782 the settlers had followed the Indians after an Indian attack on a fort near Lexington. The Indians set a trap. The settlers rode into it. Over 60 settlers were killed at the Battle of Blue Licks. The next day a larger number of settlers went to the battlefield to bury the dead. But they could not even tell who the dead were on that hot day. Some were scalped. Others had been eaten by animals. It was a sad time across Kentucky.

Harrod had been sick and unable to go to Blue Licks. When he got better he joined the army that went after the Indians into Ohio. They took the Indian towns, killed a few people, and burned crops. But their foe stayed away from a battle. The army of settlers went home, still wanting to get even for the loss at Blue Licks.

While James Harrod did fight Indians, he did so only when he had to. Some of his friends killed because they wanted to. Harrod did not, even though his brother was killed by Indians. Once when James Harrod was on a hunting trip, some Indians chased him. He crossed a river and hid behind a tree. As the three Indians crossed, he fired. Harrod killed one. He fired again and wounded a second Indian. The third fled.

Later, Harrod went back to the area and found the wounded foe. He spoke words the Indians could understand, then began to bind the wound. Harrod took the Indian to a cave. He fed the Indian and took care of him until he could walk. Then Harrod told him to go back to his tribe. Years after that, when Daniel Boone was captured, he said it was that same Indian who saved him from being killed. The Indian knew that not all settlers were bad.

Soon after the last major Indian battle in Kentucky, at Blue Licks, peace came to the area. The Indians were driven out. People began talking about forming a new state, one called Kentucky. (Kentucky was still part of Virginia at that time.) Harrod's job was done. He had settled a new land and made it safe. Other people could turn this land into a state.

Now Harrod could relax and spend time on his farm. Back at Boiling Springs, he and his wife Ann built a new home. It was said to be the first frame house in Kentucky. At about that same time, in 1785, Mrs. Harrod had a baby girl, Margaret. The Harrods both loved children. They even let their home be used as a school. Sadly, Harrod's stepson went into the woods one day to play. Some Indians came on him, tied him to a stake, and burned him. That death hit hard. Harrod closed the school. He took long trips, as before. Perhaps now he was not only hunting but also trying to forget that death.

But when he was at home, Harrod could enjoy his new house. All around it was rich land filled with crops. Slaves worked the fields. In the house itself some of the most valued things were the feather beds. They were filled with feathers from the geese on the farm. The Harrods had candles and holders for light. A spinning wheel and loom were used for making clothes. The 28 sheep gave wool for cloth. The family had about 20 cows for milk and 18 hogs for food. Honey from bees gave meals a sweet taste. The Harrods had plates and chairs enough for a dozen guests at those meals.

Harrod lived a full life. Then, in 1792, he left on that hunting trip. He never came back. That same year, in June, Kentucky had entered the union as the fifteenth state. But the man who had made the first settlement in Kentucky had disappeared.

What happened to James Harrod? Three answers are possible:

1) Because of problems at home, he took off on his own. He just left and told no one.
2) He was killed by a person in his hunting party.
3) He died in the woods as the result of an accident.

Now *you* are the historian. Which do you think is the correct answer? Here is the evidence for each one:

1) *Problems at home.* In those days, it was very hard to get a divorce. You had to have a law passed at Frankfort to get one. Only a few people each year ended their marriages that way.

Some people said later that Harrod left as an easy way to end his marriage. A lot of people took those so-called "wilderness divorces."

Was Harrod unhappy? About 50 years after Harrod disappeared, a man went across Kentucky talking to old people. He asked them about the early days and wrote down what they said.

A man named Henry Wilson said that Harrod had felt his wife was too close to some other men. Harrod told Wilson before he left, "You will not see me here again." Wilson stated that after Harrod disappeared, someone claimed to have seen him in the North. That is what Wilson remembered 50 years later. Another man said he too saw actions that showed Mrs. Harrod was not always a loving wife.

But both these men made a lot of mistakes in other things they said. Were they wrong on this, too? Or were they right?

One more thing supports the idea that Harrod did not die on that hunting trip. His wife later remarried. But the marriage proved to be very unhappy. She sought divorce. She asked that her marriage be ended because "her former husband, James Harrod, was living at the time of her marriage." In 1804—12 years after Harrod disappeared—she got the divorce.

Was Harrod alive then? Had she seen or heard from him? Probably not. She likely used that as a simple way to get out of an unhappy marriage.

But what about what the other people said? Could Harrod have left because of his wife?

There are some facts that show Harrod loved his wife. In the will he made out just before he left, he gave his land and house to his "beloved wife" and the daughter who bore his name. Other people said "he almost worshiped" his wife Ann.

Those who supported Mrs. Harrod stated that she was smart and had a strong will. She would not give in to anyone if she felt she was right. Her friends said all the stories about her years later came from people mad at her. Those people had made up and spread mean gossip.

Were the rumors true or false? Did Harrod leave on his own, or did he die? Which person do you believe?

2) *Harrod was killed.* Mrs. Harrod always stated her belief that her husband had been killed on the hunting trip. She told people that a man named Bridges asked her husband to go search for the silver mine. Mrs. Harrod did not trust Bridges. She warned her husband. Harrod said he was not afraid, but he did make out a will. A third man went with him and Bridges.

Later, at camp, that third man said he heard a shot. Bridges came back and said Indians were in the woods. When Harrod did not return, the two men then left. They went to Lexington. Bridges soon sold some furs and silver buttons in a shop there. The owner sent the buttons to Mrs. Harrod. She said they were her husband's.

Harrod's friends went looking where Harrod had last been seen. In a cave they found some bones. One person said they also found a shirt with the buttons gone. But other writers state that there was no shirt. No one knew if the bones were Harrod's or not. But when Harrod's friends got back, Bridges had fled. Mrs. Harrod believed they had found her husband's body in that cave. Her son-in-law and two other people said about the same thing 50 years after that.

But Mrs. Harrod also gave a different story later.

Under oath she swore that James Harrod "was killed or died in hunting and he has not been heard of since, a part of his clothes being found in the river." Were those Harrod's clothes by the bones in the cave? Or were Harrod's clothes in the river?

If his friends found bones that they felt were Harrod's, why didn't they bring them back to bury? There is no known grave with James Harrod's name on it. Did Bridges kill Harrod and hide the body? Or did Harrod's friends find the body of an Indian or some old, forgotten trapper instead?

3) *Death by accident.* Sometimes the simplest answer is the best. Perhaps Harrod just had an accident in the woods and died as a result. If his clothes were found in the river, he could have fallen in and drowned. Or he could have fallen from a cliff and been killed. Or he could have been hurt and unable to walk. He might have gone to a cave for protection and been killed there by wild animals. Or he could have been shot by Indians, as Bridges said. Harrod was about 46 years old at the time. He may simply have died of natural causes.

Ann Harrod never remarried after her divorce in 1804. She lived by herself until her house was burned. Her daughter died before she did. By then Mrs. Harrod had lost her parents, both children, and two husbands. In 1843 Ann Harrod died at the age of 88. She never knew for certain what happened to James Harrod.

Do we now?

Tecumseh

This and the following two photographs are courtesy of the Harrodsburg Historical Society.

# Who Killed Tecumseh?

A legend may have only a little truth to it—or a lot. In 1813 a great Indian leader died. His name was Tecumseh (TA-KUM-SE or TA-KUM-SA). His life would become legend.

The legend told of a tall Indian man with light skin. This Indian fell in love with a white girl. She taught him how settlers lived. She read to him. But he would not give up his Indian way of life, as she asked. They did not marry. But he left as a changed person. Later, Tecumseh's men would never kill women or children. Nor would they kill prisoners. Tecumseh became a great and brave chief. He dreamed of uniting all Indians. A good speaker, he was a born leader. Even his foes liked him. He fought them fairly. But he could not defeat their much larger forces. He died trying. So goes the legend.

In truth, Tecumseh was not overly tall—only 5 feet 10 inches. Nor was he different in his copper coloring from any others of his tribe. Nor do facts support the story of his love for a white girl. And he was not always brave—he ran away in his first battle.

Yet much of the rest of the legend was true. A great chief, Tecumseh led his people—these Native Americans—in an effort to drive back the hated new Americans. But his final fight with his foes only added to the legend. He died. But no one knows how he died or who killed him. There are many questions but few real answers.

Some parts of Tecumseh's life are known; some are not. He was born a Shawnee Indian in about 1768. When he was only 6 years old, his father was killed fighting the whites. (That was the same year James Harrod first settled in Kentucky.) At the age of 11, Tecumseh saw his mother, a Creek Indian, leave him and go west. An older sister then raised him among the Shawnee.

Growing up, the young Tecumseh lived a life like most boys of his tribe. Shawnee tied their babies to boards to make sure the babies grew straight. Every day mothers washed their children in cold water to make the babies strong. Parents made children listen to the older people and respect them. Games taught children how to shoot and jump and run.

Indians needed such skills, for the Shawnee both hunted and farmed. Men hunted for food to eat and furs to trade. Women farmed and cooked. No one owned the land they farmed. People helped each other and shared their wealth.

Most of the time the Shawnee lived in towns. Their wood and bark homes could not be moved. The Indians cooked outside. In the winter both men and women wore buckskin pants, buffalo or bear hide robes, moccasins, and hats. During the summer women wore cooler, looser tops. Men wore no shirts and only a breechcloth. Bright feathers and paint added color to their outfits.

The Shawnee were religious people and felt that the Master of Life had made them. If Indians lived as the Master of Life wanted, they would be happy, they said. An Evil Spirit lived also, and the Shawnee said he made bad things happen, often through witches. This was Tecumseh's world as a youth.

As Tecumseh grew up, his world changed. The Shawnee began to buy goods from settlers and forget their own crafts. They traded furs for pots and pans or for clothes. Many old Indian ways were forgotten.

As settlers came west they said the land was their land, not the Indians'. The settlers killed the animals. They gave the Shawnee alcohol, and drinking became a problem. New diseases, such as smallpox, killed more Indians than did any gun. Some Indians did not fight the new ways very long, and they "walked the white man's road." But other Indians, such as Tecumseh, would fight the new ways. These Indians tried to save their people's old way of life.

Tecumseh's tribe had always moved a great deal. Some Shawnee lived in the South, some to the East. Tecumseh's tribe likely lived in Ohio at the time of his birth. No Indians then lived in Kentucky. But Indians saw that land as theirs. They hunted in Kentucky. The whites had another view. To them, no one lived on that land, so it was free for them. The two groups—Indian and settlers—soon would fight over that land. The "free" land had a high price in lives.

Tecumseh hunted some in Kentucky. On one such trip his horse fell and broke the young boy's leg. One of Tecumseh's brothers stayed with him until the leg healed. That brother, like Tecumseh's father, would soon be killed as he fought the settlers.

When he was 15, Tecumseh joined older braves and attacked a settler's boat on the Ohio River. He fought well. The Indians took a prisoner and later burned that prisoner at the stake. Tecumseh did nothing. But he said he would never again let a prisoner die.

Tecumseh became a war chief by 1790, when he was about 22 years old. His brother's death made him a fierce leader, for that brother had been like a father to him. Tecumseh led war parties to drive out the settlers. But he was fighting a losing battle. At a place in Ohio called Fallen Timbers, in 1794, American soldiers defeated the Indians and killed another of Tecumseh's brothers. Many Shawnee then made peace. But not Tecumseh.

After the battle of Fallen Timbers, Tecumseh went back to his tribe and married. He ended that marriage soon after and married again. His second wife bore him a son, but his wife died later. He did not marry again and saw little of his son. Tecumseh now watched as still another of his brothers did what Tecumseh wanted to do—unite the Indians.

The Prophet

Tecumseh's brother became known as the Prophet. Blind in one eye, once a heavy drinker, the Prophet did not seem like a leader. But he said he had had a vision. The Master of Life had told him that the settlers came from the Evil Spirit. The Shawnee must end their trade with the settlers. The white man's ways were wrong, said the Prophet. Indians must not drink the white man's drink or use the settlers' tools.

The Prophet said that if the Shawnee did as he said, then the great days of past years would return. Animals would come back to the woods. Crops would be good. The land would be free once more. Soldiers would fall before the Indians' power.

What the Prophet really gave Indians was a new religion of hope. That religion would bring order to the

mixed-up world the Indians faced. The Prophet made
the Indians see their fight as one of good against evil.
In 1806 he told the tribes that he would make "the sun
to stand still." An eclipse of the sun did happen. Many
Indians then said that the Prophet spoke for the Master
of Life. Indians from many tribes joined this holy man.

Tecumseh became the war leader, his brother the
religious leader. The Prophet got the Indians to unite,
while Tecumseh tried to make them ready to fight.
Tecumseh also tried to get British support. He knew he
would have to fight a large force from the United States
some day and would need much help.

Tecumseh began to travel all over the South and
Midwest to try to get other Indians to join him. But for
hundreds of years, Indians had fought Indians. Some
tribes hated another tribe more than they did the
settlers. Tecumseh had a hard task.

Yet Tecumseh was a good speaker and leader. The
U.S. General William Henry Harrison met Tecumseh
and felt his power. General Harrison said that the chief
had been working for years to unite all Indians.
Harrison stated that if the United States Army had not
been around, Tecumseh would already be the leader of a
great Indian nation.

Tecumseh's hope for a united Indian force took him
again to the South. He tried to get other tribes to join
him. But while Tecumseh was gone, his brother made a
mistake. The Prophet told the Indian forces that

soldiers' guns could not harm them.  He said the Indians should attack General Harrison and his men.

The Indians tried to surprise the soldiers at the Battle of Tippecanoe with an attack before dawn on November 7, 1811.  For two hours the fighting went on.  Almost 200 soldiers were wounded or killed, and the Indians had about the same losses.  Finally, the Indians left the field.  They blamed the Prophet for their losses.  His power was gone.

Tecumseh got back two months later and tried to rebuild his forces.  He grew very angry at his brother.  But soon after that, the War of 1812 began and Tecumseh started to get British support as they too fought the forces of the United States.

At first, the war went well for the British and Indians in the West.  The U.S. forces gave up at Detroit and later lost a major battle as well.  Tecumseh had won a smaller fight.  With only 24 men, he hid by a stream.  About 150 soldiers rode into view.  The Indians fired.  The surprised soldiers ran, with 19 dead and 12 hurt.  Tecumseh lost just one man.

Tecumseh also fought beside the British.  In one such battle, he was shot in the leg.  As he got better, however, the U.S. forces grew stronger.  In April 1813, the British and Indians tried to take an Ohio fort.  General Harrison led the U.S. soldiers, who stayed behind the fort's walls.  The general knew more men were on the way.  Those new U.S. forces surprised the

British and Indians and made them run. But Tecumseh got his men and fought back. Of the 800 new U.S. soldiers in the attack, only 150 got to the fort.

The U.S. prisoners had to run between two lines of Indians. Many were killed. More were killed by Indians inside the British camp. Tecumseh heard of the killing and rode to the camp. There he told the Indians to stop. But 40 soldiers had died. Tecumseh grew very angry and blamed the British for not stopping the killing. Back at the fort, the Indians and British later left. With General Harrison and his forces inside, the fort was too strong to take.

A few months later, the Indians and British made an attack on a smaller fort, also in Ohio. The leader of the U.S. troops, from Kentucky, was only 21 years old and had just 200 men. His foes had many more. But the soldiers would not give up. The Indians saw that the fort would be hard to take. The British tried and lost 100 men. The U.S. lost 8. The British left the fort alone after that.

The two tries to take the two forts lost Tecumseh some Indians and support. His men needed to win again to build up their spirits.

General Harrison had more men now and moved forward. The British began falling back into Canada. Tecumseh was ready to fight. The women and children with his men were tired and could not go on much longer. Tecumseh told the British leader they must stop

William
Henry
Harrison

and fight the U.S. soldiers soon. So the British and Indians made ready at a place near the Thames (TIMS) River. It was October 4, 1813.

That night in the U.S. camp, General Harrison made his plan. He had fought the Indians before at the Battle of Tippecanoe and at the fort. He knew he faced a tough foe. Meanwhile, others also made ready. Sixty-three-year-old Colonel William Whitley had been one of the first people to settle in Kentucky. His big home in Lincoln County still stands. He had fought the Indians before, also, and had lived. But this time Whitley told a friend he expected he would be killed.

Tecumseh knew the battle would be the real test of his forces. If he won, he might unite the Indians. But he too felt he would die the next day. Tecumseh said, "I shall never come out. My bones will lie on the battlefield." His father and two brothers had died at the hands of the whites. He would fight to the end, as they had.

The day of October 5 opened sunny and clear. The U.S. men recalled how Indians had earlier killed some people after the battle at the River Raisin. There the U.S. soldiers had given up. The British had said the soldiers would be safe, but then the Indians had killed the unarmed men. Now, at this battle, the cry would be, "Remember the River Raisin."

The British and Indians watched as the bigger U.S. army came toward them. Then the battle began. On the right side of the field, the British lines broke in five minutes and the soldiers fled. On the left side, however, the Indians had a better place to fight from. The Indians also had more spirit.

The U.S. troops were mostly men from Kentucky. Ahead of them lay Indians hidden in some brush, trees, and logs. The soldiers wanted to send 20 men out first to draw the Indians' fire and see where the Indians were. While the Indians reloaded their guns, the rest of the army would then attack. But the 20 men might be killed. They knew that. Yet they agreed to go. The army called these 20 men the Forlorn Hope.

The 20 men moved forward to within 15 yards of the Indian line. Shots rang out. Smoke from the guns covered the field. Many of the Forlorn Hope were shot. Those left charged into the large Indian force. Then the rest of the soldiers moved up. They cried, "Remember the River Raisin." One of the Forlorn Hope was Colonel Whitley. He saw an Indian rise up behind a log. Colonel Whitley shot this Indian, but then another Indian killed the old Colonel. Kentucky soldier David King took the Colonel's gun. At that moment, a friend of his called for help. King turned and killed an Indian with Whitley's gun.

The leader of the 20 men had been Colonel Richard Johnson of Scott County, Kentucky. Seated on his white horse, Johnson was shot several times as he charged into the Indians. His horse was hit by 15 bullets and finally fell. Just then, an Indian chief ran toward the wounded Johnson. The chief raised his tomahawk to kill him. Johnson took out a pistol and shot the Indian. Other soldiers took Johnson back to be cared for.

Of the Forlorn Hope's 20 men, 15 had been killed and 4 more hit. But they had done their job. The whole U.S. army now fought the Indians. But suddenly the Indians fell back. Word spread that Tecumseh had been killed. The Indians fled. The Battle of the Thames was over in less than an hour. The U.S. forces had won.

But what exactly had happened? Who had killed Tecumseh?

Some facts are clear. The soldiers attacked and in the fight Tecumseh was killed. His Indians said he had

Colonel Richard M. Johnson
Courtesy of the University of Kentucky.

been dressed in plain clothes, not like a chief. Tecumseh had been shot in an earlier fight and had a bandage on his arm. But that is about all that is clear.

At least four answers can be given to the question "Who killed Tecumseh?"

1) *Colonel Whitley.* This old Indian fighter died in the battle, so he could not say what happened. Almost 30 years later, two soldiers said that Whitley shot an Indian behind a log. The body was later said to be Tecumseh's. The dead chief had a bandage on his arm, they stated. Some 60 years after the battle a famous Kentucky historian said that "Whitley probably did kill him."

2) *David King.* About 20 years after the fight, one man told how Colonel Whitley was killed by an Indian, and how then Colonel Whitley's friend Private David King shot that Indian. Another soldier told how a soldier called for help and with Colonel Whitley's gun King shot the attacking Indian. Later the person said to be Tecumseh was found, shot, where King had killed those Indians. At least one of the dead Indians, however, was dressed in the fine clothes of a chief. An early historian wrote only three years after the battle that some dead Indians lay where Tecumseh was killed "and Mr. King . . . had the honor of killing one of them." Was it Tecumseh?

3) *Colonel Johnson.* At that time Richard Johnson was a member of Congress. He never said that he killed

Tecumseh, but his friends did. That claim helped him win elections. His enemies tried to defeat him by saying the claim was false. So his part of the story gets mixed into politics.

In Johnson's own words: "I put myself at head of . . . 20 men, and we advanced . . . . We received the whole Indian fire . . . . The rest of the troops came up and we pushed forward . . . . I noticed an Indian chief . . . . He fired upon me." Johnson was hit in the hand, his fifth wound. He stayed on his horse. Most of the rest of the men were on foot.

Said Johnson of the Indian: "He came out from behind the tree and advanced upon me with uplifted tomahawk . . . . I drew my pistol and . . . fired, having a dead aim upon him. He fell, and the Indians shortly . . . fled." Johnson said that he had killed an Indian leader. He did not know if this leader was Tecumseh.

Three days after the battle a man wrote his father and gave the same story. "I saw an Indian rushing on Johnson when he was down, but he managed . . . to shoot the Indian . . . . Tecumseh was shot directly in the left side of the breast . . . . I looked at him after his death." Five years later a British historian wrote that Johnson killed Tecumseh.

Several Indians supported that story. Anthony Shane was an Indian who had taken an American name and fought on the U.S. side. He was one of the few people at the battle who knew Tecumseh. Shane is said to have told people that he went to the spot where Johnson killed the chief. He saw Tecumseh there, dead. Indians told him that a man on horseback had killed him. Shane looked at Tecumseh's wounds. They seemed to have come from Johnson's pistol.

Another chief with the Indians said he saw Tecumseh killed by a man on a white horse. But when Johnson was pointed out to him later, the chief said Johnson was not the man. Two other chiefs stated they saw a man on horseback shoot Tecumseh with a pistol.

4) *An unknown soldier.* Two other Indian chiefs said they saw Tecumseh get killed. Their story is not the same as that of the other chiefs. They said their great leader fell on the first fire from the U.S. forces. Still another chief, Black Hawk, said the same thing. He stated: "At the first discharge of their guns, I saw Tecumseh stagger forward over a fallen tree . . . . He was killed."

One person said he spoke to Anthony Shane about six years after the battle. At that time, Shane told him a different story than he later told others. Shane said Tecumseh was shot by a Kentucky army private. Two Indians near Tecumseh during the battle had told this story to Shane.

Did Whitley, King, Johnson, or someone else kill Tecumseh? Each of the first three men killed an Indian, all in about the same place. Was one of those Indians

Tecumseh? Or was he killed by a stray shot from somewhere else?

Another question is what happened to Tecumseh's body. That is a mystery in itself. Just like the question of who killed the chief, that question has many answers.

The most common account said that a body was pointed out as Tecumseh's. Angry soldiers scalped the body and then skinned it. But a different story was that they did not get the right person and the real Tecumseh's body was not touched. His body was taken away later and buried.

In fact, soldiers at the battle gave three different accounts later. One wrote: "It was Tecumseh's body they skinned, I have no doubt. I knew him . . . . My men covered it with brush and logs and it was probably eaten by wolves." Later a different man said he got people to describe Tecumseh. Then the man looked at that body and it was the chief's.

But another person said he saw Indians carry away Tecumseh's body at night, and it was not harmed. A third man also said the body was not harmed and that he himself buried Tecumseh, on General Harrison's orders.

Yet not one of these people knew the great chief. Only General Harrison and a few others had seen him. The general looked at a body said to be Tecumseh's and could not say if it was Tecumseh's or not. Another man may have told people the wrong body was Tecumseh's, since he knew what would happen. He did not want the chief's body to be torn apart. Tecumseh was too great a leader for that.

Even the Indians do not agree. Most of them say Tecumseh's body was not skinned, but that another chief's, near it, was. Black Hawk stated that he went back the night after battle and took away Tecumseh's body. He buried Tecumseh in some nearby woods. But two other chiefs said that Tecumseh was taken away as soon as he was shot. They buried him four or five miles away. Another Indian said the body was taken away only two or three days after the battle.

To add all this up, then:

1) Some people said they looked at a body said to be Tecumseh's in one place, some in another place.

2) Some state one body was Tecumseh's and that this body was scalped and skinned. Some say another body was his and that body was not touched.

3) Some say Tecumseh's body was carried away and buried by Indians, but no one agrees on the time or manner. Others say the body was buried on the battlefield by the soldiers.

As one historian said, "No one knows how he was killed, who killed him, or where he lies buried."

41

In short, then, the only thing people agree on is that Tecumseh was killed. If we do not know where he was killed, how can we know who killed him? If people cannot even agree on the same body, how can we expect them to agree on who did the shooting? And if so many persons disagree on such basic points, how can any of them be trusted? If you were a historian, what would *you* say if someone asked you, "Who killed Tecumseh?"

The results of Tecumseh's death were no mystery, however. His attempt to bring all Indians together against the settlers and soldiers had failed. He would be called a noble leader. But his cause and his vision were no more. In the future Indians—Native Americans—would still fight. Yet after Tecumseh, their hopes for victory would never be so great.

Within 20 years after his death, the Shawnee had moved across the Mississippi River. They left their hunting grounds in the East for all time. Thirty years later, the Shawnee were placed on reservations in what is now the state of Oklahoma. There they had little control over the future. Theirs would be a very different future from what Tecumseh wanted.

Of his foes that day at the Thames, Colonel Whitley was buried in a blanket near the river. General Harrison became president in 1840, due in part to his role in the battles at Tippecanoe and the Thames. Richard Johnson became a senator and in 1837 vice president of the United States. His slogan in the election had been:

Rumsey Dumpsey
Rumsey Dumpsey
Colonel Johnson
Killed Tecumseh.

But no one knew if he had or not.  The legends live on.

James W. Tate

From *The Biographical Encyclopaedia of Kentucky* (1878).

# The Fate of "Honest Dick" Tate

The laws of Kentucky are based on the state
Constitution. One of the parts of that Constitution says
that the state's leaders can serve only one term of
office. Then they have to leave that office for at least
one full term. Only a few states have that limit. Most
states let people serve more than one term. Kentucky
has that rule because of a man named James W. Tate.
Few people have heard of him. Who was he? What did
he have to do with that rule? And what happened to
him?

The people of Kentucky loved James Williams
Tate—for a time. He was a native of the state, born in
1831 in Franklin County. His father was a farmer; his
mother was the daughter of a preacher. Tate himself
began to work at age 17 as a clerk in the post office.
Later he became an aide to the clerk in the Kentucky
House of Representatives.

In 1867, when Tate was 36, he ran for state
treasurer. He won. For the next 20 years he served in
that post. The treasurer took care of all the state's
money. Every two years Tate ran for the office. Every
two years he won. The state's leaders were his friends.
The voters felt he did a good job.

Tate seemed happy. He and his family lived in a
nice, new home on Second and Shelby streets in

Frankfort. In 1878 a book on state leaders stated that Tate was "upright in his dealings." He was said to be honest, a man "of the highest order." Voters called him "Honest Dick" Tate. He had everything going for him.

Nothing seemed odd on March 14, 1888, when Tate went on a brief trip to Louisville. He packed his bags and left quietly. In Louisville he stayed two nights and watched a stage show. The next day he got on a train for Ohio. Tate was never seen in Kentucky again.

Back in Frankfort, state leaders began to worry. A week passed. Finally people began to look at Tate's accounts—his records. What they found shocked them. "Honest Dick" Tate had fled Kentucky with a lot of the state's money. He was a thief.

It took a long time to find out the exact details. A group looked at his records and finally was able to give their report. First of all, Tate kept very bad records. His letters were all over the rooms, in no order. Bills had been paid but not marked "Paid." Other bills were forgotten, it seemed. The group needed ten days just to sort it all out. In the final report, the state of Kentucky came up $247,000 short—which would be the same as more than ten times that amount today.

Tate had been able to take that money because no one really checked his records for those 20 years. The people who were to do so never did. They trusted Tate. Nor did the legislators look at his records, even though they were to do so as well.

Tate had been a friendly person. When some judges or other officials needed money or an advance on their salary, he would give it to them. They signed an I.O.U. These loans were not legal. The sums loaned ranged from $1.85 to $5,340. Some paid the money back. Some did not. The state thus lost. But those leaders did not want anyone to look very closely at Tate's records. No one did until it was too late.

Some of the money the state lost just came from the fact that Tate was careless with his funds. He kept money in all kinds of odd places, including little purses and bags. People found $1,000 in cash behind a safe. The money had fallen out and had gotten mixed in with some trash there. No one knew it was gone because of Tate's poor records. In short, some of the missing money did not go to Tate.

But Tate did use his post for his own gain. "Honest Dick" used the state's money as his own to buy land in other states as well as coal mines in Kentucky. On the day Tate left, a clerk in the treasurer's office saw him stuff two big sacks full of gold and silver coins. Tate also took with him a large roll of bills. It is likely he fled with up to $100,000 in cash.

When all the details were finally sorted out, the state acted. They first had to remove Tate from office. That is done by the rare process of impeachment. An impeachment simply says that the official may be guilty of a crime and should be tried. The Kentucky House of

Representatives quickly issued articles of impeachment. Then the Kentucky Senate acted as the court to decide if Tate was guilty.

For three days, witnesses came before the Senate. The governor told that he had planned to have Tate's records looked at and that Tate probably fled as a result. Detail after detail came from others. Then the vote was taken. Tate was found guilty. He was removed from the office of treasurer.

But the story does not end there. Two years later, a group met to change Kentucky's Constitution. Out of their meeting would come the state's present Constitution.

One matter they talked about was whether a state official should be elected by the people or selected by the governor. They decided on an elected office. Then they had to decide if the person could be re-elected. On that question, the "Honest Dick" Tate affair loomed over them.

One person stated that an official should serve only one term: "Perhaps the longer he stays there the more he steals." Others called Tate a "rascal," a man who "was elected too much. They [other officials] cannot learn the tricks so well in a short time."

Not all agreed. Other people said that a one-term limit meant a good leader had to leave, or that sound officials could not serve their state for long periods of time.

But, in the end, the example of Tate won out. In 1891, the people voted to limit most officials to one term. Even though most states no longer have such a limit, Kentucky does. "Honest Dick" Tate is still having an effect on Kentucky.

But where did the 57-year-old Tate go? What happened to him? In some historical cases, as with Harrod and Tecumseh, there is too much different evidence. All kinds of "facts" have to be balanced to find the truth. In the Tate case, the problem is not the same. Here too little is known. More evidence is needed.

Tate left for Cincinnati that March day over a century ago. He left behind his wife and daughter. Years later they said they got letters from Tate for a time. He had gone north to Canada, then west to the Pacific Ocean. Tate then went by ship to Japan and China and back to California in the U.S.A. One man said he saw a letter from Tate that had been sent from Brazil two years after Tate left. If so, that was the last heard from "Honest Dick" Tate.

What happened to him after that? Did he return to the U.S.A. and live here under another name? Or did he live out his days in South America, using the state's money? Did he think about his family or his state? Did he regret what he did? And, finally, how and when did he die? Did some thief in a far-off nation notice this rich man and kill him for his money? Or did he die a quiet death, forgotten and unloved? Does James W.

Tate lie in an unmarked grave in an unknown country? If anyone knew the answers to those questions, he or she said nothing. Tate's fate is still unknown.

What is known is that his crime was not forgotten. The people who made Kentucky's present Constitution did not trust officials because of Tate. Tate's bad example overcame the many good examples which could have been used to allow officials to serve longer. Even after death, Tate cast a long and dark shadow over Kentucky.

# The Case of William Goebel

Up to this point in this book, the stories have shown that some parts of history have no simple answers. That is one of the lessons of history—learning that many problems in life are complex and do not have clear-cut answers. The stories of Harrod and Tecumseh, for example, showed that sometimes there can be several answers and that some writing is the opinion of one certain writer.

Yet, much of history is based on facts. Facts are matters about which no one would disagree. This chapter looks at a man to whom something happened that has happened to no one else in American history. We will try to find out what is fact and what is not in his case.

William Goebel was born in 1856. His parents had come to America from Germany. Their son did not speak English until he was of school age. By then, the family had moved to Covington, in northern Kentucky.

Goebel grew up poor and later recalled how he stood barefoot in the snow, selling papers to earn money. But he was a good student and did well in school. Goebel soon became a lawyer, then went into politics. He was elected to the state senate.

At that time, a change was taking place in Kentucky. The old leaders came under attack. One

William Goebel

Courtesy of the Kentucky Historical Society.

state official—"Honest Dick" Tate—had fled the state with about $247,000 missing from his accounts. Some people said the old leaders were not honest and were stale. New ones were needed to give a fresh outlook. Other voters said some big businesses ruled those leaders. Those voters wanted reform also.

Goebel wanted to lead the young reform forces. By 1887, when he was elected state senator, he was only 31 years old. Goebel had become known as the poor person's friend. He defended some poor people in law cases and did not charge them fees. But he became rich by attacking big businesses in other law cases.

In politics, Goebel had a hard time gaining power. He was not a strong speaker and did not show a lot of humor in public. The fact that he attacked the old way of doing things made some voters unhappy, too. So to gain power, Goebel became a "boss." He made deals behind the scenes. Goebel would offer jobs for votes and do other things to gain support. That made some voters distrust him. Others disliked him a great deal for other reasons.

In 1895, he met one such angry person, John Sanford, in the streets of Covington. A newspaper that Goebel owned had printed some harsh things about Sanford. The two men met, got close to one another, and then two shots rang out. A bullet went through Goebel's coat. Sanford stood still for a moment, then fell forward. He had a bullet in his head. Sanford died that night.

The two shots—one from each man's gun—came at almost the same time. No one could say which man drew his gun first. So Goebel went free. But his enemies saw him as a killer.

As the years passed, Goebel gained more and more power. He became a leader in the state senate. Then, in 1899, he got his party's support for the office of governor. But many people, even in his party, still did not like him. The race would be a close one.

When the votes were counted, it seemed that Goebel had lost his race by only 2,000 votes. His opponent was sworn in as governor in December 1899.

But Goebel's party had more votes in the legislature. The party decided to look at the election results. Perhaps some votes had not been cast properly. If so, those votes could be thrown out and Goebel would be made governor.

That was where things stood on January 30, 1900. It was a tense time, and harsh words filled the air. Goebel's opponent was in office and believed that *he*—not Goebel—had been elected and thus should serve. His party saw Goebel as trying to steal the election. The 44-year-old Goebel felt that his enemies had stolen the election in the first place and that he should get what was fairly his.

The legislature was meeting to talk about the matter

when Goebel left his hotel to join them. He never got there. Cries of "Goebel has been shot" filled the halls of the capitol.

The assassination of Goebel
*Cincinnati Enquirer,* January 31, 1900.

The following are three accounts of the events of that January day in 1900. As you read these accounts, try to answer these questions:

1. *Who* was there?
2. *What* happened?
3. *When* and *where* did it happen?
4. *How* did it happen?
5. How many shots were fired and from where?
6. Where was Chinn?
7. What did Goebel say after he was shot?
8. Who shot Goebel?

The first account, from a newspaper, came out the day after the shooting. It reads:

On January 30, 1900, William Goebel was shot by would-be killers. Tonight he lies near death, shot by a rifle bullet. The would-be killers were on the second and third floors of the Executive Building and five shots were fired from the windows. The shot which hit Goebel came from a second-story window.

Mr. Goebel was on his way to the Senate, with Jack Chinn and Eph Lillard. Goebel and Chinn were walking side by side. Near the capitol building a shot rang out from a large three-story building, the Executive Building, some fifty feet away.

As the shot was heard, Goebel fell to the ground. Several more shots were heard. None of them touched him. Lillard went to aid Goebel, who was supported by Chinn.

"Get help," said Chinn and then asked Goebel:

"Are you hurt, Goebel? Did they get you?"

"They have got me this time," said Goebel. "I guess they have killed me."

The second account is from a court trial that same year. Eph Lillard, who was with Goebel, said: "I heard a gun crack on my right. It came out of the Executive Building. I could not see it. I turned quickly and saw one of the windows up. It was the second window from the corner on the lower floor. I suppose the shot came from there."

Jack Chinn, also with Goebel, said: "I was by Goebel's side. When he fell, I said, 'Goebel, they have killed you.' I heard five more shots. Then I said, 'Lie down, they will shoot you again.' Goebel answered, 'That's right.' "

Later that same year a book came out about the shooting. The book was based on accounts from many papers and from many people. That work said:

On the morning of January 30, Eph Lillard, Senator Goebel, and Jack Chinn went up the walk toward the capitol; Lillard went ahead and Chinn dropped back, being winded by his walk from his hotel. Chinn said:

"When we were about half way between the fountain and the capitol steps, I heard a rifle.

"At almost the same time, Goebel bent over, fell

to his knees, and I said, 'My God! Goebel, they have killed you.'

" 'I guess they have,' he said as he was falling.

"I said, 'Lie still Goebel or they might shoot you again.'

"The first shot struck Goebel and it was fired from one of the upper floors of the Executive Building. The first shot was followed by four others, and I heard the bullets hum by me. Soon some men came out and we took Goebel to the hotel."

Now go back over the eight questions on page 56 and answer them.

While the other stories in this book often show that there can be many answers to the same questions of history, on some questions certain "facts" exist. In the Goebel case, all the accounts agree on certain things, including answers to these questions:

1. *Who was there?* Goebel, Lillard, Chinn, and the person or persons who shot Goebel.

2. *What happened?* Goebel was walking toward the capitol when he was shot.

3. *When and where did it happen?* On the morning of January 30, 1900, in front of the capitol.

4. *How did it happen?* A rifle shot came from the Executive Building and Goebel was hit.

These could be seen as the facts of the case, the facts of history. All the accounts agree on these answers. But answers to the other four questions are different and varied. It is harder to find out the facts in answering these questions.

5. *How many shots were fired and from where?* The newspaper said five shots, as did the book, but in the trial, Chinn said six. The shots, said the newspaper, came from the second floor. Lillard, at the trial, stated the shots were from the first floor. The book, using Chinn's words, said Goebel was shot from one of the top floors.

6. *Where was Chinn?* In the newspaper story and in the trial, Chinn was said to be beside Goebel. The book presents him as being behind Goebel.

7. *What did Goebel say after he was shot?*

| Newspaper account: | "They have got me this time. I guess they have killed me." |
| Trial account: | After Chinn spoke, Goebel said, "That's right." |
| Book account: | After Chinn spoke, Goebel said, "I guess they have." |

8. *Who shot Goebel?* The accounts here do not say.

Based on other accounts in the trial and in other places, most people said Goebel was shot from the first floor of the Executive Building. That was important, because a man whose office was on that floor was later tried for the crime. The number of shots is really not important; only one hit Goebel. Nor is it important where Chinn was. (Likely he was behind Goebel and did not admit that.) Also, Goebel's words simply show that Chinn, the only person who heard them, recalled them different ways at different times. The real question was—and is—"Who shot Goebel?"

Three people went to jail for the shooting. But in the trials the juries were not picked fairly. Many people had doubts that those in jail were guilty. Later, two different governors agreed and gave the men pardons. The best answer to the question "Who shot Goebel?" is, "We do not know."

What happened to Goebel, who had been shot in the chest and lung? The decision was made that he should have been elected governor in the first place. Goebel was sworn in as governor. Three days later he died, on February 3, 1900, the only governor in American history who died in office as a result of a shooting. He had lived only four days after the shooting. The opposite political party had not agreed that Goebel should have been made governor. They did not give up the office and took the case to the U.S. Supreme Court. The court ruled in Goebel's favor, long after his death. The matter was over.

Today, Kentucky has a new capitol. But the old one still stands in Frankfort, and a spot in front of it shows where Goebel was shot. Goebel's coat, with the bullet hole in it, is on display in a museum there. And in front of the Old Capitol stands a statue of Goebel. All is now quiet and peaceful on those once-bloody grounds, but those who walk by still ask, "Who killed Goebel?" No sure answer can be given them.

Another mystery of history remains unsolved.

The Seal of Kentucky—revised.

*Minneapolis Journal,* February 1, 1900.

# Other Readings

*On Harrod:*

Thomas D. Clark, *A History of Kentucky.* Lexington: Bradford Press, 1960.

Kathryn H. Mason, *James Harrod of Kentucky.* Baton Rouge: Louisiana State Univ. Press, 1951.

*On Tecumseh:*

R. David Edmunds, *Tecumseh and the Quest for Indian Leadership.* Boston: Little, Brown, 1984.

Jerry E. Clark, *The Shawnee.* Lexington: Univ. Press of Kentucky, 1977.

*On Tate:*

Hambleton Tapp and James C. Klotter, *Kentucky: Decades of Discord, 1865-1900.* Frankfort: Kentucky Historical Society, 1977.

Emmett V. Mittlebeeler, "The Great Kentucky Absconsion," *Filson Club History Quarterly,* vol. 27 (1953).

*On Goebel:*

James C. Klotter, *William Goebel: The Politics of Wrath.* Lexington: Univ. Press of Kentucky, 1977.

*General:*

Robin W. Winks, editor, *The Historian as Detective: Essays on Evidence.* New York: Harper, 1968.

# About the Author

A native Kentuckian, James C. Klotter grew up in the eastern part of the state. He attended the University of Kentucky and received a Ph.D. from that school.

Dr. Klotter is currently the State Historian and assistant director of the Kentucky Historical Society. He is the author of numerous books and articles about Kentucky and the South.